Selections from

ROBERT SCHMANN

ALBUM FOR THE YOUNG OP.68

Piano Solos by Master Composers of the Period

Editor: Dale Tucker
Art Design: Joann Carrera
Artwork Reproduced on Cover: *Knitting* by Albert Anker

CONTENTS

ROBERT SCHUMANN

Born: June 8, 1810, Zwickau, Germany
Died: June 29, 1856, Endenich, Germany

Robert Schumann, youngest of five children in his family, was born in Zwickau, Saxony (Germany) June 8, 1810. His father was an author, publisher, and bookseller who became ill the year young Schumann was born. Schumann began school and his first music lessons in 1816 and studied piano with a local church organist. Over the next few years, Schumann was taken to music recitals and his first opera, all of which had an influence on him.

In 1829 he became a student at the Zwickau Lyceum and during his eight years there grew to be an accomplished pianist. Schumann also showed great ability as an author and wrote articles and albums of verses and poems, which were compiled and sold in his father's shop. By 1821 he was playing for performances of oratorios and produced his first compositions for choir and instruments.

In 1826 Schumann lost his father and only sister, both having suffered for years. Two years later he completed his schooling and went, against his wishes, to the University of Leipzig as a law student. During these years he traveled with friends and continued to compose, influenced by the music of Beethoven and more so that of Schubert. Several piano sonatas and intermezzi grew from this period. This same year, Schumann began his study of piano again as a student of the respected teacher Friedrich Wieck. By 1830 Wieck persuaded Schumann's mother to allow him to cease his study of law and concentrate completely on music. Through Wieck, Schumann was introduced to Chopin, Mendelssohn, and Moscheles, who also influenced his writing. During the next three years, Schumann actively composed, producing a large amount of piano music. Several of his larger sets came form this period, including *Papillons* and *Carnaval.*

September 12, 1840, Schumann married Clara Wieck, daughter of his former teacher and a concert pianist in her own right. There had been a serious interest between the two for years, much against the wishes of Friedrich Wieck. Many of Schumann's piano and vocal works were dedicated to or inspired by Clara, and she persuaded him to compose chamber and orchestral music also.

Schumann often suffered from severe depression during his adult life and regularly turned to alcohol to offset his problems. The deaths of family members, friends, and admired composers would send him into deep depression for extended periods, as did separations from his wife when she traveled to perform. In 1852 he suffered a rheumatic attack, which sent him into another period of depression and failing health. His compositions from this period reflect his solemn moods, and at this same time he began having difficulty working with other musicians. Later that year, Brahms visited Schumann, which was the beginning of a friendship and an inspiration to Schumann.

As his mental health deteriorated over the following years, little music was written. Schumann lost his primary conducting position, but Clara continued to travel and perform. Schumann attempted to take his own life several times and was committed to doctor's care soon after. He spent his last two years separated from his wife but was often visited by Brahms and Joachim. Schumann died the afternoon of June 29, 1856, and was buried in Bonn, Germany.

MELODY

Opus 68, No. 1

ROBERT SCHUMANN

Moderato

SOLDIER'S MARCH

Opus 68, No. 2

HUMMING SONG

Opus 68, No. 3

Allegretto

A LITTLE PIECE

Opus 68, No. 5

Andante

THE POOR ORPHAN CHILD

Opus 68, No. 6

HUNTING SONG

Opus 68, No. 7

Allegramente, con freschezza

1) Performed as a grace note in this period, just preceding the beat.

THE WILD RIDER

Opus 68, No. 8

Allegretto

THE HAPPY FARMER

Opus 68, No. 10

Animato e grazioso

SICILIENNE

Opus 68, No. 11

1) Schumann's pedal markings.

2) Performed as grace notes in this period, just preceding the beat.

cresc.
f
Presto
p
D.C. al Fine

KNIGHT RUPERT

Opus 68, No. 12

Allegro

Tranquilo
p
cresc.
sf
p
fp

51
f
sf sf sf
56
sf sf sf
61
sf sf sf
66
sf sf sf
ff
70
ff

FIRST SORROW

Opus 68, No. 16

A LITTLE ETUDE

Opus 68, No. 14

Leggiero ed equale assai

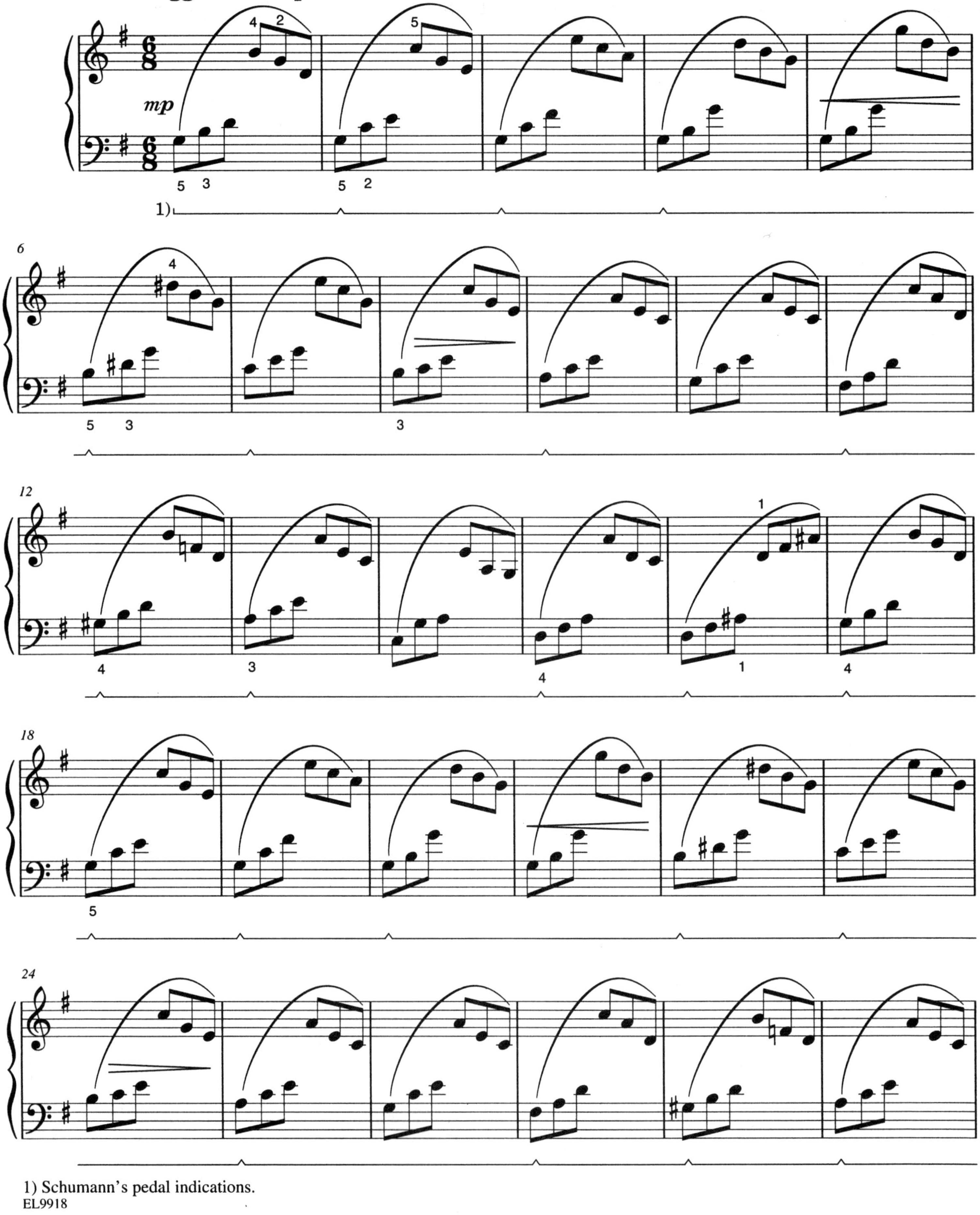

1) Schumann's pedal indications.

*Schumann's own alternate performance suggestion.

THE REAPER'S SONG

Allegro ma non troppo Opus 68, No. 18

1) Performed as grace notes in this period, just preceding the beat.

A LITTLE ROMANCE

Opus 68, No. 19

Non presto

1) Schumann's pedal markings.

RUSTIC SONG

Opus 68, No. 20

Moderato

1) Schumann's pedal markings. 2) 

THE HORSEMAN

Opus 68, No 23

Breve e deciso

REMINISCENCES OF THE THEATRE

Opus 68, No. 25

Un poco agitato

dim.
cresc.

UNTITLED PIECE

Opus 68, No. 26

Moderato, con grazia

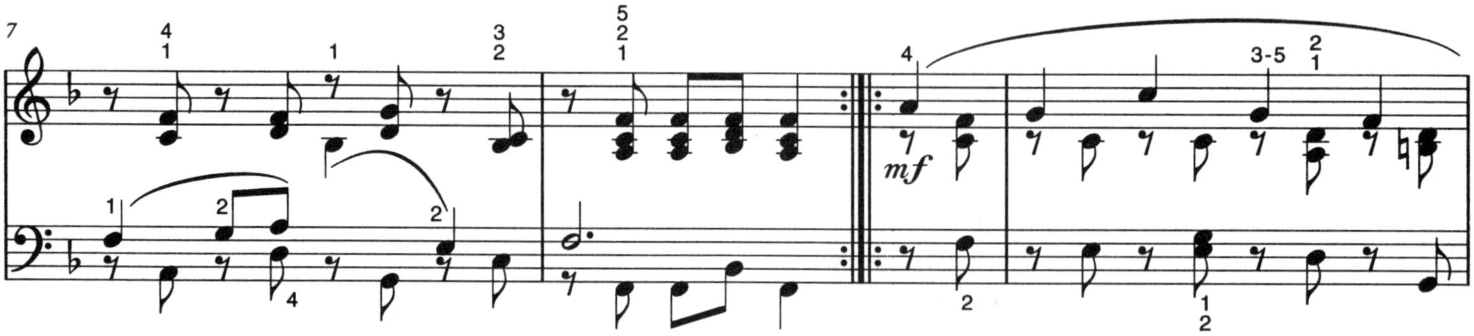

1) Performed as a grace note in this period, just preceding the beat.

Un poco più lento
fp
p
a tempo
fp
fp

THE STRANGER

Opus 68, No. 29

Energico

1) Schumann's pedal markings.

sf
sf
sf
sf
sf
Coda
p
cresc.
pp
f
ff

ITALIAN MARINER'S SONG

Opus 68, No. 36

1) Performed as a grace note in this period, just preceding the beat.

sf
fp
cresc.
fp
sfz
(p)
cresc.
sfz
p
sf
sf
fp
cresc.
fp
Lento
Presto
sfz
f
pp
f